D0063063

Nearly 20 years after her death, Joan Mitchell looks to be the only artist of her generation, man or woman, who produced a big, abstract, painterly painting that can stand up to the best of de Kooning and Pollock. The legions of arrogant young men who swaggered into the Cedar Tavern have been eclipsed by this woman who probably had more self-confidence and certainly had a more abundant gift than any guy her age in the room.

—Jed Perl, art critic, *The New York Times Book Review*

BLUE
TERRITORY

a meditation on the life and art of Joan Mitchell

ROBIN LIPPINCOTT

www.TidalPress.com

Published in the United States by Tidal Press.
Learn more at www.TidalPress.com.

Cover photograph by
Stacey Evans Photography.
Cover design by Laura S. Jones.

ISBN: 978-0-9846617-8-7

for the love of Joan!

In a society that didn't allow abstract painting she would have gone to jail.

—Barney Rosset on Joan Mitchell

If Mitchell had had to choose but one color out of which to make a rainbow, it would certainly have been blue. Whether the blue that makes darkness visible, the blue of water, the blues in Cézanne, van Gogh, and Matisse, the blue of morning glories or delphiniums, or 'the blues' of jazz and sadness, blue was critical to the life of Mitchell's painting.

—Klaus Kertess, *Joan Mitchell*

PREFACE

At Harvard's Fogg Art Museum, I ask to see the
two pastels and a screen print of Joan's in their
holdings. The attendant brings out the first
pastel and leans it against an easel. It is framed
(white wood), and the use of pastel is so varied
that at times it appears liquid, like paint. Forest
green, royal blue, turquoise, black, and rust are
the colors, but they are fully exploited; in places,
the rust is so faded or rubbed out that it appears
rose-colored.

This pastel, the attendant tells me, is from 1959.
Down in the lower right-hand corner, I spot her
signature: the *J* in Joan a straight line, a mark
that is repeated in the last *l* in Mitchell (the first *l*
having been made with the traditional elongated
loop).

The screen print is labeled *Untitled (Blue Sky)*
and dated 1959-60. Also recorded is that this

print is from *The Poems*, perhaps those of John Ashbery she created work for? It is mostly blue and black.

For the other pastel, a second attendant accompanies me to a locked and darkened room, turns on the light, and walks to a stand of vertically stashed works, looking for the call number that matches the one written on the slip of paper in his hand. What he pulls out is a pastel from 1980, twelve years before her death. It features a rainbow of colors, scrambled and scribbled, almost nest-like. These clusters dominate the top and bottom of the page. The marks in the middle are lighter and less distinct. And once again there is a lot of blue.

Her signature has changed slightly; now, both of the *l*'s are parallel lines, formed in a way that makes them almost indistinguishable from the *J* of Joan. Looking at the signature closely, again and again, I can't help but also notice the slight space between the first syllable of the last name and the second. *Mitchell. Mit chell.* In German, *mit* means *with*, and one definition of *hell* is *bright*. In English, *Mitchell*, the syllables unified, is a surname which derives from the name Michael, meaning *Who is like God.*

Also at the Fogg, I see Cézanne's *Study of Trees*, from 1904, and I recognize that my approach here seems much like that of Cezanne's representation of trees: a study.

JOAN

JOAN, JOAN—the name alone as fully resonant as the sound inside of a drum (under the skin), or in the inner ear; bone deep (deep as the ocean and as wide and vast as a windblown Midwestern sky); a tone poem or a koan; room to roam, and yet also contained (within the frame of *J* and *N*)—not unlike her paintings. Reverberant, and also spelled J-h-o-n-e, English form of Johannes; Old French feminine form of Johannes. There is the initial entry consonant J (a shovel-full), followed by the sheer wide-openness of that strong, long vowel, O (a lonesome wolf howling), the silent, embattled A, and then the resounding but not overly emphatic N (a dark piano chord), which issues a finality, a soft-pedaled closure to the name. It is womanly, somehow mournful, rhymes with moan, and yet it is also insistent, and finely honed—perfectly fitting for, and fitting perfectly, the woman at hand.

And so in the end she is always Joan, simply Joan, but a Joanier Joan—the Joaniest, one for the Ages—our own Joan of Art.

BIG JOAN/ LITTLE JOAN

She is a woman you will never see without a cigarette between her fingers or her lips—until it is too late (the cancer); and a drink, preferably Scotch, and much later wine, is rarely very far away from the other hand—when it is not holding a paint brush. Because of *how* she paints, actively, she will be always slim, forever fit, with broad shoulders, strong arms and torso, and thin, shapely legs. There is the unvarying mop of brown, shoulder-length hair atop, bangs brushing characteristically raised eyebrows. And there is that wry, shy smile. Later, there are the oversized, face-obscuring glasses: it is all about hiding, and seeing—she has been far-sighted since age three. Many will say that she has the mouth of a sailor, that she is tough, irascible. In France they will call her *sauvage* (as both van Gogh and Cézanne were *sauvage*): in her case because she is direct, says what she thinks, is not careful or diplomatic or, as she defines it, hypocritical—lying, really. But she is also an innocent, downright girlish: Big Joan/Little Joan is how she explains herself to herself—with the help of a few psychiatrists: Big Joan goes out into the world and travels; Little Joan stays home with her dogs and paints.

She admits to being afraid of death. Her father dies, her mother dies, and then her sister dies. Countless beloved dogs, perhaps the loves of her life, die, too. Abandonment is also death, she says, and her longtime lover ("my twenty-four year live-in" is how she refers to him), abandons her for the dog-sitter. She never says Good-bye and forbids her friends to say it. Somebody comes for dinner and later they leave. In her mind, they have already left before they have come. She begins to dread Good-bye at Hello. It is the reason, or one of the reasons that she loves painting, because in paintings there is stillness. There is no time and so there is no death.

SKATING

She is alone and skating on ice. She listens as the silver blades slice and scratch the surface, watches crystalline shavings scatter and glisten in the furtive winter sunlight, leaving a trail of white flakes in her wake. The grooves she makes form patterns, a kind of calligraphy: she is cutting figure eights. She loves the turns, the swerving curves, the elegant arcs; on the ice she is all fleetness and grace, free. Late afternoon, Garfield Park, downtown Chicago: she is sixteen years old. The year is 1942. The sky is big and bluish and open, shot through with white—an overturned bowl; but the light, which has a certain metallic quality, gilt-edged by the weak winter sun, is beginning to fade. For the time being, her feet, her legs are one with the ice, and in this way she is grounded, connected to the watery earth beneath. Ten years later, in New York, De Kooning will tell her that some of his happiest childhood memories are of skating along the canals around

Rotterdam. Twenty-five-plus years hence, in her studio in Vétheuil, thirty-five miles north of Paris but still overlooking the meandering Seine, she will more than once remember these times on the ice, this feeling, these movements, and the messages that she cut with her blades, a choreography of her own—all of which are not unlike what she experiences when she paints, brushing a broad, continuous swath across a canvas that is much higher and wider than she is tall. One long, sustained brushstroke, followed by another, and then another, and so on, and after a time and several changes of brushes, sudden short jabs, a frenzy of quick, learned, wrist-flicked strokes and fingersmears, a deliberate smudge or a rubbing here, something scumbled, and then a few drips there, gestures in various colors, a furious cluster of paint—all of it controlled. As she works, legs apart, her extended hands and arms become a part of the very air. From a distance (the other end of the studio) she resembles a dark starfish splayed against the canvas, always reaching, stretching—and like a starfish she cannot be easily pried away from whatever she attaches herself to, in this case painting: for she is finally free, freely creating, and regardless of the source emotion, it is almost impossible not to feel joy in the act.

But all that is in the future. Now let us return to this moment in downtown Chicago, Garfield Park, when she is sixteen and skating on the ice under this leaden sky. You have no idea of all she will go through in the years between now and then, and of course, neither does she. Soon, the sun will fall too low in the sky and she will have to skate to the side of the rink, sit down, put on her wooden skate guards, and clomp off the ice and back into the quotidian, returning to her family and becoming, once again, mere pedestrian—all of which will be witnessed by these bare trees, which stand sentry: it is as if they are watching her. But for now, she continues to traverse the ice. Pressing down into the toe of her boots, hard, she loves the full stops, loves cutting into the ice, the incisions, a kind of surgery or wound. She deposits most of her desires there. For now.

A girl, her foot shod in metal ending in a sharp point, digging its way forever into one piece of earth. In fact, she was erratic and self-contradictory, and her real fascination lies in the way that these contradictions did not end in the stillness and silence of her death.

—Mary Gordon, *Joan of Arc*

THE ALPHABET
IS COLOR

I am trying to imagine her life...

She lived a full sixty-seven years, and if we break it down, arbitrarily but neatly, divide that life into thirds—the first part ending when she was twenty-two, the second at age of forty-four, etcetera.

I can easily imagine the middle period—painting in New York (and also Paris) in the context of that famously macho, alcohol-fueled art scene in the late 1940s through the '50s: we'll go there later. I can also readily access the last third of her life—living and painting at the place she bought in Véthueil, in and out of her relationship with Riopelle, the Canadian painter—until he leaves; surrounded by her beloved dogs; then beset with health problems for much of the final decade (gum cancer and two hip replacement surgeries, before the lung cancer that killed her), but still and always (up until the very end) painting, and drawing with pastels. We'll also see her there. As for the first part of her life—

She is born in Chicago in 1925. Her father is a doctor and amateur painter, a very self-made man. Her mother is a writer, more specifically a poet, and an editor (with Harriet Monroe) at *Poetry*. She has an older sister (Sally) by two years. Though her childhood envelops the years of the Great Depression, her family is protected because of her father's profession and also because of the untouched wealth accumulated by her mother's father, a German émigré and an eminent engineer, a builder of steel bridges—a structure that will fascinate her all her life: bridges cover water, span voids. Thirty-eight movable bridges arch across the Chicago River.

The family apartment overlooks Lake Michigan. Picture them now at the dining room table on a long winter's night—chandelier blazing overhead, their faces reflected in the great plate-glass window. A large barge chugs slowly along on the ice-choked lake down below. Snow is falling. The silent foursome sits in dim light, amid their mouthfuls.

Turn the scene out the window upside down, and the chunks of ice become frothy cumulus clouds, and the sky transforms into blue, the blue waters of summer.

Now shake the scene, and the flakes of ice atomize into snow, forever falling out the family window.

For the adult Joan, the scene is malleable; she takes it with her wherever she goes, transforms it, makes it her own. It is a white memory—white is snow, cold, ice, and silence (her mother's luminous pearls, her sister's perfect teeth, her father's stiff shirt): white is not light.

But there is also the field of blues, various shades of blue—sometimes the sky, or the lake in summer: "bluer than bleu" as she will say later in France. Blue territory.

Words are made-up of color; the alphabet is color. These are memories and feelings that will be with her, and that she will paint again and again, throughout her life; experiences that cannot be put into words—"If I could say it in words, I'd write a book."

Draw back inside of the window now, into the apartment itself, and what you find is not the warmest of households: her father is a very busy man, and he is also an older father—in his late forties when she is born. Her mother, also busy, and probably somewhat remote by nature (a poet, after all), goes deaf seven years after her second daughter is born, the same year that daughter begins to paint. Later, Joan will say that she often tried to imagine what it was like to be in her mother's head; that she wanted to share her mother's silence. At age ten the future painter writes a poem, the last line of which reads:

"And bleakness comes through the trees without sound."

JOAN ALONE

Joan alone—in her bedroom, a girl of seven, painting after dinner on a Saturday evening: the light is not good but she does not yet know about the importance of light. At the Art Institute earlier today, one of her classmates painted a map of the state of Michigan—green for land, blue for water, and said that it looked like a glove. But Joan disagreed and said *No, it is a palette*, and then the classmate cried that Joan would not recognize her painting for what it was. Joan just stood there and looked at her, amazed, bemused even. She will paint for the rest of her life.

Joan alone—in her bedroom, age ten. She has retreated here because she and Sally have been fighting again—over the alphabet this time, or to be more precise: when Joan informed her sister that every letter of the alphabet has a color—*A* is green, *S* is red, and so on, Sally shook her head and said, *No, it doesn't*, and she asked Joan, *Why?*

and she wanted to know *How?* Joan knew this, *How she could be so sure?* Joan just shrugged and said that *it just is and always has been*—that's all. Alone now, she begins to write out the word-colors that are in her mind....

Joan alone—in her bedroom, fourteen years old, smoking, painting, and depending on the turpentine (which she uses liberally) to hide the smell of cigarette smoke from her parents. She is trying out oil paint, working on a landscape from a *plein air* excursion that she made with her father last weekend. If only he didn't always have to ask whose was best? Why does one always have to be better than the other? Why can't they just be different? Why must *everything* be a competition? Years from now she will remember this moment as the genesis of her move toward abstraction: that way there would be no comparing.

Rebel

with a Cause

Joan and Sally fight often during these early years—ostensibly about color and its relation (or lack thereof) to words, but really about so much more; only later do they become close. Sally, who is blond and pretty and extremely social, goes to a proper school with a proper Nancy who will later become Mrs. Ronald Reagan. Whereas the Rebel Joan *just says No* and opts to attend the progressive and unconventional Francis W. Parker School, both a grammar school and a high school, near Lincoln Park.

"Full of Jews," she will say later, adding that Chicago is very racist, an epithet she also hurls against her own parents.

But there are good times with her parents, too. Outings with her father, for example: they go to the zoo, or to the Field Museum to draw. It was with him that she first painted *plein air*.

During a sledding adventure on the shore of Lake Michigan, father pulling her, mother watching from on high (trapped behind silence and glass), Joan somehow falls off the sled, into the water, and disappears. Because she is wearing an eye-catching red beret, she is spotted and saved: vivid color comes to the rescue—and not for the last time. Her mother blooms in the window above.

Her father is a very straight-laced, conventional man who, having failed to produce a male heir he had planned to name John, pushes and coaxes and coerces his youngest daughter—his last, best hope—to excel, and thus to carry on his name. This is, after all, a man who donned a black hood in order to treat Al Capone's syphilis: St. Valentine's Day Massacre indeed! That was the crime-ridden Chicago of Joan's childhood.

Out of a desire to please her father, young Joan becomes a championship figure skater, an award-winning diver, and a heralded tennis player. But she also becomes resentful, because her aging father, now in his mid-sixties, is competitive *with* her, even when they paint together; she comes to feel sure of his love only when she is winning medals and awards. Before long, all she will want in this world, the one and only thing, is to be free of him. And soon, though not soon enough, she will achieve this through painting, particularly abstract painting, when (she comes to realize) he can't even criticize what it is. Only then will she feel protected.

But Joan's father also provides her with the will to succeed, and with a strong work ethic and drive—the training wheels that prepared her for the male-dominated art scene of New York in the '40s and '50s.

Whereas her mother gives her the word, *poetry*— something that will sustain her throughout her life.

Her mother's writer friends, for example—Thornton Wilder, Edna St. Vincent Millay, T. S. Eliot and Dylan Thomas—all stop by the apartment; the author of *Our Town* frequently reads to the young Joan. It is a very literary household—full of books.

Her mother is also, as Joan will put it later, "a split woman": she has been a writer, suddenly a wife, then a mother of two, and she can't reconcile the three. Joan becomes a mother to her deaf mother. She longs to escape—not from her mother, whom she later calls "a tender and sensitive companion," but from her fate: she does not want to become a second-generation split woman. She will strive for the rest of her life to be whole, something she achieves through painting.

Her work will be noted for its lyricism; many of the titles of her paintings will come directly from poems—"Hemlock" (from a line in Wallace Stevens' "Domination of Black"); "To the Harbormaster" (Frank O'Hara). Etcetera. She develops an early and sustaining love of Wordsworth (*The world is too much with us*), Wallace Stevens, T. S. Eliot, her beloved Rilke. And after she leaves Chicago, she will befriend and collaborate with many poets in Manhattan, brethren of the New York School—O'Hara, James Schuyler, John Ashbery.... Somewhat later, in Paris, Jacques Dupin will be another collaborator; and there is also her friendship—and possibly more—with Samuel Beckett.

Joan has her first exhibition at the age of twelve, showing casein paintings at the Parker School, where her classmates include the future writer and artist Edward Gorey, and the future cinematographer and director Haskell Wexler. As a result of frequent trips to the Art Institute with her father, by the age of sixteen she has already seen the work of van Gogh (her first love), Matisse,

Cézanne, Manet, Goya, Titian, Chardin, Soutine and Kandinsky, her eyes filled with and widened by their canvases, their shapes, their colors.

At the Parker School, one of her teachers introduces her to the boldness of Kokoschka, and also opens up the world to her by delivering the message that to be an artist you have to go through poverty and passion. Passion she knows already—she feels things deeply (everything, it seems); poverty is alien to her, but she will work hard to try to get to know it later, down and out in New York and Paris. It is because of this teacher, Joan will say later, but also just because of how she is, that she turns her back on convention.

Another classmate at Parker, Barney Rosset, later (and briefly) becomes Joan's one and only husband (but a lifelong friend). He will also be the founder of Grove Press, the *Evergreen Review*, and act as Samuel Beckett's American agent. He describes Joan then as defiant, aloof, and already hard at work on her painting. To which he adds that she was also all muscle, both in body and attitude.

PAINTING

In 1942 her gouaches of landscapes become increasingly eccentric in their deployment of color: she is growing, squirming, all elbows as a teenage painter, bursting at the seams of representation. In one painting, stripes of the most vivid hot pink and saffron yellow dominate an otherwise ordinarily rendered horizon. They're just *put there*. It is as if painting what she sees, or what she thinks she's supposed to see, is beginning to inhibit her. Or perhaps better put: she is beginning to paint what she sees and what she feels in just the way that she sees and feels it.

She finishes high school early. Her father thinks that at sixteen she is too young to go to art school. She wants to go to Bennington. He tells her that it is *too arty*.

Sitting in the train car on her way to Smith College in Northampton, Massachusetts, she passes the bleak, steely war factories in Gary, Indiana.

"You carried death around with you to the extent that you were sensitive" is how she has described that time.

At Smith she majors in English. It is fall 1943 and WAVES march on the green in Northampton.

She paints watercolors out under the apple trees, walks around Paradise Pond. There's a lovely Goya in the museum there. And she *wants*, she is always wanting, and then wanting more. But more of what? A bigger life...

Painting saves the day. But throughout her life she will have a writers' deep reverence, respect and love for words.

She spends the next two summers at Oxbow, an art colony in Saugatuck, Michigan, run by the Art Institute of Chicago. She blossoms there— the nude is painted outdoors in the mornings; landscape classes outdoors in the afternoon, and lithography at night. No electricity, just oil lamps.

"Really Frenchy" is how she remembers it.

At Saugatuck, age seventeen, she takes her first

lover. She finds she can lose herself during sex in a way only previously possible when she was painting.

But it is the *entirety* of the Saugatuck experience that impresses itself upon her, becomes indelible; for the rest of her life she will recall and draw upon the Saugatuck landscape as from a well—the dunes and the birches, the greens and yellows, and the blues, *Oh! the blues*—the ruminating continuum of Lake Michigan, the particular color of the lake there being different from any shade of blue she ever saw from the window of the family apartment in Chicago.

Many years later, her métier as a painter will be her ability to distill landscapes through the agency of memory.

"I carry the landscape around with me," is how she put it. "Sort of packed in a suitcase. Over time, the suitcase gets bigger...."

Leaving Chicago

"I left Chicago in the middle of the night with a man in a station wagon" is how she described escaping the hometown she had returned to—that man being none other than Barney Rosset who, being a Jew, her parents snubbed.

They had first met when Joan was in eighth-grade and Barney in tenth. She recognized a fellow rebel—he was obsessed with the Spanish Civil War at the time; he was also charmingly Chaplinesque. Two years later they went on their first date, to see *Citizen Kane*. The war separated them. But by 1947, both were smitten; Joan joined Barney at his Brooklyn Old Fulton Street apartment, almost under the Brooklyn Bridge.

Now, wandering Manhattan on her own, Joan visits the museums and galleries, where she first sees the work of Gorky and Pollock. Gorky's muscular-yet-fluid style is what appeals to her (and what she learns from), not his surrealist imagery. She is simply not ready for Pollock—not yet.

She walks languidly through the city streets, any time of day or night, often wearing a trench coat and sometimes seemingly in slow motion. Years later she might have been tracked by Truffaut's hand-held camera, perhaps to a score by Miles Davis. *Follow her*:

Streetlights and gutters. Gargoyles and opera. Button shops and peep shows: Cornell's utopia.

It's a different kind of light. The light of the northeast. In a city like no other. Sunlight trapped in the canyons of buildings and shot down the long avenues with the focus and intensity of a spotlight. The softer, late afternoon light. And evening light (softer still). At night, it's never completely dark. Morning light—dawn, quiet and hushed. The light that comes after rain. Gray, New York City light.

There's color and movement, too. And noise. Take her future painting *Evenings on Seventy-third Street*—it's all there. So many of the paintings from this time, mid-to-late fifties, have it—that speed/sound/color/movement/rhythm, contained chaos.

And then there is the varied (and variegated) landscape of Central Park. She wants to paint it, or not *it* but how it makes her feel, what she remembers....

She studies Kandinsky's early paintings, his feeling and fluidity. And she is also thinking a lot about Mondrian and his grids—repeatedly asking the staff at the Guggenheim to allow her to study its collection of his work.

Training her eye, and her hand.

And though she has been excited about attending Hans Hofmann's class, she goes once but leaves before it is even over, later saying that she couldn't understand a word he said, and also that she was terrified.

"He was talking about the push and pull, and he was erasing people's drawings."

But she likes his paintings very much, and later the two will become friends, and in what will become something of an art historical moment, passed down in anecdotes, she will encounter him in Washington Square Park (one early morning), walking her dog George (see "George Went Swimming at Barnes Hole, but It Got too Cold"), and he will doff his hat and say to her,

"Mitchell, you should be painting!"

Living in Brooklyn, under the bridge and by the river, she is finally away from home, away from her father, free—or so she thought would be the case. But now there is someone else to get away from, to struggle with, to push and pull against: she and Barney live in such close quarters. And there is also the river (more water). It is too intimate—too close too much too soon—and they fight often.

For Barney, Joan is mysterious and compelling; he doesn't fully understand her psychology, and yet he is more in love with her than she is with him. More than once, he proposes to her and she turns him down. A filmmaker and a photographer at the time, he takes some lovely nudes of Joan that document his feelings for her; one could very well be a still from a French film, Jeanne Moreau, or perhaps a young actress portraying Jeanne d'arc:

She is lying in bed, holding a pillow, her body turned toward the camera but her face looks away and down. She appears as if she may have just woken up—fresh and tousled.

Suddenly, Joan is a woman of twenty-two. The first third of her life is over.

MEXICO

Nobody talks about Mexico, Barney said. *Mexico was very important.*

That was '45, '46, when Joan went to Guanajuato, outside Mexico City, with a friend, and the two sought out the famous muralists José Clemente Orozco and David Alfaro Siqueiros. Orozco told them that Matisse was the best painter in the world.

But the colors of Mexico, and the scale of Orozco's work—those are things Joan took with her, put in her suitcase and unpacked for the rest of her life.

"I had been in love with Mexico, you know."

PARIS

In the spring of '48 she travels alone to Paris for the first time, on a Liberty ship, having won a fellowship to paint abroad. And though one might be inclined to picture a liberated Joan of Art standing proudly at the prow of the ship as it plows through the onrushing and disobedient water, this Joan sleeps on deck in a sort of tool shed, primed with booze from the crew; the green-paint of the surface comes off on her feet.

She arrives in Le Havre, just as the sun is setting. Ships, still sunk from the war, litter the harbor. It is horrible. Ugly. Dark red, Goya-ish. And all she can think about is war and blood and war—*war is screaming!* There are shortages; just about everything is being rationed.

She finds a studio for four dollars a month on rue Galande, across the Seine from Notre Dame. Her toilet is a hole in the floor, there are rats, the coal stove is smoky and there's only a single light bulb for electricity, but she is getting to know poverty. And the view includes one of the oldest churches in all of Paris, St.-Julien-le-Pauvre.

Philip Guston, a generation before her, and Sam Francis, a Californian with whom she has a brief affair, are there, along with other American expat painters, and that helps; but now she misses Barney. She writes and tells him that the people are so poor: "(T)hey don't seem to laugh at all—only walk with their heads down, brown bread tucked under their arms because there is no white bread... I think so much of the war when I'm not thinking of you—of people with courage & no stockings...." She says that the lower East Side of Manhattan is luxurious in comparison. She also tells him of her walk to Sacre Coeur, and to Montmartre to see Picasso's first studio there.

Despite the view from her own studio window, she hates her work; she doesn't know what to paint or how to paint it. She's doing semi-abstract work, and executes what she knows at the time will be the last figure she will ever paint—one with no features and just the most rudimentary of limbs, a final dismemberment of sorts: she's just not feeling it. After that, she will remove the figure entirely and keep on "Cubing it up," as she puts it.

Endless, agonizing hours, days, weeks, months pass, time spent staring at the blank canvas, with the knowledge that she is on her way to something but not there, she has not arrived; it is frustrating having to wait, not knowing where she is going, how or if she will ever get there. It is, she realizes (dipping into the zeitgeist), *existential*.

That July, Gorky commits suicide; she'd learned so much from his work early on, and recognized a kindred spirit. It's another plunge backward and downward, a kind of vertigo that has become all-too-familiar. Her living conditions are making her ill and a doctor advises that she go south. Now Barney rejoins her and the two move into a friend's house in Le Lavandou, Provence, a house once owned by Gide. Joan passes the rest of the year painting and pacing, or not painting and pacing, pacing and smoking, feeling lonely and fighting with Barney—

She runs out of money. Once again, Barney asks her to marry him; he's besotted. He says he'll pay her way home if she'll marry him but not if she doesn't, adding that he'll also carry her paintings back to New York. Reluctantly, because she knows her only true partner is painting, she agrees; the Mayor of Le Lavandou cries *Vive Chicago*! The newlyweds arrive in New York City on New Year's Eve, 1949.

MANHATTAN

The Chelsea Hotel on 222 West Twenty-third Street is Joan and Barney's first home. Before too long though the itinerant couple picking up and moving into their own Manhattan digs, a tiny dollhouse near the White Horse Tavern on West Eleventh. In the spring, Barney comes down with hay fever, so he and Joan go to Haiti, and then to Cuba (Barney's father knows Battista). But now there's a hurricane coming their way, so they fly away from it and to the Yucatan.

Back in Manhattan that fall, the two have to move yet again, but Barney has stayed on in Mexico City. Mike Goldberg, a fellow painter, helps Joan move from Eleventh to Ninth Street, between Fifth and Sixth. In the spring of '51 she leaves Barney for Goldberg and moves into a bare studio with a coal stove on Tenth Street where Philip Guston, also returned from Paris, lives just above.

These are the peripatetic years—the rapid and sometimes rabid rhythm of searching about for *something*, but not finding it, the *it* being not quite who or what you're looking for and so you just continue looking, seeking really, which also requires moving about: you have to have faith, to know you'll know it when you see it. And all the while Joan is increasingly starved for other painters (Barney was always with film people), just ravenous, and for one painter in particular: Willem de Kooning. That's what she's looking for—or rather *who*. There was a painting of his, a big black and white painting that spoke to her, at the Whitney, probably "Excavation": such mastery! She has never heard of de Kooning before (*Who is he?*) but now she wants to meet him, *has* to meet him. She has to find a way.

The first studio she goes to is Franz Kline's, and there are all of these, well, *Klines* is what they are, and they're un-stretched and hanging on the brick walls, and WOW! they're just beautiful: those large, bold swaths of black and white paint evoking steel bridges and other urban structures. And there are the telephone book drawings all over the floor, too, and Kline is going on and on in that way Joan later comes to know he always does—warm and generous and larger than life....

The next thing she knows, eight or ten hours have passed and it's already morning and they have talked the night away—or rather *he* has talked the night away (she's happy to just sit there and listen), and she is crazy for it, crazy for it all: *it's fantastic!*

And then she finally finds de Kooning, locates him in his studio over on Fourth Street.

Bill, he tells her to call him.

He works on a single painting all that winter long. She goes up there, looks for herself and says, along with the chorus, *Why doesn't he stop? It's finished!* But it isn't. And he doesn't. And only he seems to know what he's doing. But she really digs it.

"I'd listen and we'd drink," is how she later describes the time with de Kooning and Kline.

Then she gets involved with The Artists' Club, one of the very few groups that accepted women—for $35 a year. And it is at "The Club" that she meets Frank O'Hara.

Everything Joan did was colored by the accident of her femaleness, like a foreign accent that inflects every syllable and determines the interpretation of every word. We would respond to a man with Joan's career in a way so different from the way in which we respond to her that it would be unrecognizable.

—Mary Gordon, *Joan of Arc*

THE

OBSTACLE RACE*

Joan, if only you were French, and male, and dead, I'd show you—is what one gallery owner said to her at the time.

Eventually she can laugh about it—and does. But she couldn't see the humor then: it was too serious, too important.

At the time, what it felt like was ... an assault, like she was being pelted with words. It hurt, deeply, made her feel as though her very being was a violation, that she was all wrong. Or that was one strain of her feelings. The other was a determination to show what she could do, and so she imagined each letter of those thirteen words as a color, and the words themselves as paint, and then she tried to think of something or someone she loved, because she knew if she could just turn it around, if she could just do that one thing, then she'd have a new painting going:

she'd pour it and drip it and smudge it and smear it and rub it and slash it and gesture all the way to China and back. And then she would have won, because when she's painting, she can forget herself; she can cease to exist. And that's bliss!

* The title of Germaine Greer's treatise on "The Fortunes of Women Painters and Their Work" (Farrar Straus Giroux, New York, 1979).

STILL A SMALL
WORLD FOR WOMEN

"What was it like to be a woman in the macho '50s? Do you mean, am I a feminist? I am. But I really like painting, whoever does it."

"Well, you got shows in those days through men. In fact, the people who encouraged me were always men. They inspired me and encouraged me."

"The men helped me more than the women. It's still a small world for women and they're cutthroat with each other."

"When I was discouraged, I wondered if women really couldn't paint, the way all the men said women couldn't paint. But then at other times I said, 'Fuck them,' you know?"

"The galleries had quota systems—no more than two women to a gallery.... "

"I would have had a lot easier time, had a lot more security, assurance, if I had been Joe instead of Joan."

"Frankenthaler? You mean that tampon painter?"

THE CEDAR

She is not alone but momentarily she is being left alone, though there is a sea of other people, people sitting in booths, people standing at the bar up front, people milling about, all seemingly suspended in a sea of smoke. *Seals*—she imagines them as seals. Seal heads bobbing, awash. And they're all talking. Or barking. *Talk, talk, talk, Talk, talk, talk.* Squawking, like chickens. But Frank (1) is not here tonight sitting next to her, and so there is not someone who feels absolutely compelled to engage her, or to be engaged, every single goddamn second. And while she *loves* the intensity of that, she also needs to just sit for a moment, sit and think (or not think) and stare off into space. It is some time after two in the morning—though who ever really knows the exact time in the Cedar, because of that crazy clock with the hands that sometimes turn backward? And who really cares, with no good reason to get up in the morning? She has had a few scotch and sodas, she's forgotten how many—they just seem to come, and now she is sitting and staring at the flaking green paint. She could focus on one of the Hogarth prints on the wall and *go there*, into that world, for a while, but she'd really rather not; instead she is looking at the peeling green plaster and thinking green, *green*—a favorite color. But she can't think that: there are so many colors she loves—blue, for example; yellow; she can't have a favorite, it would be like a mother having a favorite child (hell, some do). Well, green is *A*, anyway; or *A* is green, in her alphabet of color. *A* is green and *S* is red, *S* as in Saugatuck. She remembers Saugatuck and the flood of color there, the blues and the yellows, as she shifts in her seat and thinks, *Damn these booths need new springs*, and now she looks up, grabs for her smokes, shakes one out of the pack, places the cigarette between her lips and sets it ablaze.

She suddenly remembers where she is and looks around: Mike (2) is sitting next to her, and seated next to him is Grace (3); Edwin (4) and Rudy (5) are across from them along with someone she doesn't know. Now she recognizes Kline's (6) booming voice coming from the next booth and wishes she were sitting *there*. She thinks she heard him say *Tarzan* and looks over in his direction in time to catch a flash of his moustache; she pictures Tarzan swinging on Kline's moustache. De Kooning (7) and Elaine (8) are there. And Guston (9), whom she's known since Paris; he lives upstairs from her now, and though she likes him (perhaps because they're so much alike: prickly, intellectual, full of angst), she does not like his work. And that woman Ruth (10) is there, too, the ubiquitous one that everybody says Pollock (11) is seeing, in spite or because of Lee (12); she looks kind of like Elizabeth Taylor. Kline is gesturing wildly (she laughs at her own pun), one hand holding up a beer and the other flailing about. Now, she smiles, remembers—it must have been last summer in East Hampton, walking along with him and de Kooning, and Bill pointing to the taped windows of a newly built house and saying, *Look, there's a Kline!* Now she looks up again and when she does, Mike—who is sitting right next to her, too close, within a hair's breath, really, and with those glasses of his with their thick, black frames and eternally dirty lenses—is looking back at her. It is too much, he is much too close. And so she returns to looking at the green walls and thinking about color....

(1) Frank O'Hara (1926-1966), poet and art critic
(2) Michael Goldberg (1924-2007), abstract expressionist.
(3) Grace Hartigan (1922-2008) abstract expressionist
(4) Edwin Denby (1903-1983), poet and critic
(5) Rudy Burckhardt (1914-1999), photographer, Denby's lover
(6) Franz Kline (1910-1962), abstract expressionist
(7) Willem (Bill) de Kooning (1904-1997), abstract expressionist
(8) Elaine de Kooning (1918-1989), painter and de Kooning's wife
(9) Philip Guston (1913-1980), abstract expressionist
(10) Ruth Kligman, mistress to Pollock and de Kooning
(11) Jackson Pollock (1912-1956), abstract expressionist
(12) Lee Krasner (1908-1984), abstract expressionist and Pollock's wife

HER FIRST
MASTERPIECE

It's a tree, or not a tree but the memory of a tree.
Oh, just look at the goddamn painting!

Winter swirls

clouds of limbs

elbowing their whorls—

splayings and

furious branchings

and snow   white   death

Hemlock, 1956
Oil on canvas, 91 x 80 in.
Whitney Museum of American Art, New York

George
Went Swimming
at Barnes Hole,
but It Got too Cold

In 1957, the critic Irving Sandler approaches his editor at *Art News*, Thomas Hess, saying that he wants to write about Joan Mitchell as a part of the series: *So-and-so paints a picture.*

Sandler arrives at her studio on St. Mark's Place. It is a commodious, high-ceilinged room, its space divided into two areas, the studio considerably larger than the living area. Every inch of the living area is immaculate and in perfect order as a result of Joan's compulsive nature. The studio, however, is another matter: there's paint everywhere—spattered all over the floor, sitting in open cans, oozing out of tubes, dripping down work stations and marking the walls. Gallon cans of turpentine, two-pound coffee cans filled with brushes, and dirty rags litter the floor. Something of a makeshift palette (a flat board approximately 2 x 4) is precariously balanced on a stool.

Joan wears slacks and a black sweater, and she is without makeup. She looks tired, thirty years old. Rudy Burckhardt, a professional photographer and a friend, documents the process.

Joan immediately hands Sandler a drink (scotch), and bangs her glass against his, almost as if to say—*touché*—before they have even started.

He begins the interview by throwing out a series of catchphrases, trying—in her mind—to capture her. The one to which she objects the least, she tells him, is "New York School." But she adds that she hates aesthetic labels, and then quotes Harry Holtzman's line: "Hardening of the categories causes art disease."

Sandler laughs, but almost immediately begins peppering her with questions: Is she an action painter?

"No, I spend too much time looking, which stops action."

Was Pollock an influence?

"Not much. I am too traditional."

Does she consider herself avant-garde?

"An avant-garde is by definition dated. Manifestos are obituaries. The moment something is clarified, it's dead. There is no one valid way to paint. Newness and originality as such have nothing to do with painting. I don't paint to be avant-garde or to be in history. I would like to be in the history books, but I don't set out to be."

What was it about de Kooning's and Kline's painting that gripped her?

Grips me, she corrects him. *Present tense*, she insists. Then, she does not answer. She looks away. She is thinking. And only after she has thought for perhaps as long as a minute does she respond: "Crudeness and accuracy."

With Sandler present, she begins a painting she'll call *Bridge* by stapling an un-stretched linen canvas that is ninety inches high by eighty inches wide to the wall. Because of her farsightedness she likes to work big, feels more at ease.

She tells Sandler that she is thinking about her maternal grandfather, a steel engineer who built bridges over the Chicago River.... "He wore spats, a morning coat and carried a cane.... He liked me. Neither of us spoke.... He died when I was nine." She says that she has his notebooks with all of these *fabulous* drawings of bridges.

"A bridge to me is beautiful," she adds. "I like the idea of getting from one side to another."

And so she sets to work, first sketching a central horizontal stroke, and then a whole middle area, in charcoal. Once that's finished, she turns almost immediately to tube paints and *attacks* (Sandler's word) the canvas with housepainters' and artists' brushes, with her fingers and also with rags. She works quickly. And while she employs a full range of colors, it is dull oranges and dark blues (almost black) that predominate.

Hours pass. And then a full day, as she allows the picture to sit. She resumes painting the following evening, working slowly, and frequently surveying the canvas from as far away as she can get.

"I paint from a distance. I decide what I am going to do from a distance. The freedom in my work is quite controlled."

He recalls and makes a note of what the critic Leo Steinberg has said of her work: [*Mitchell*] *has the ability to score triumphantly for the willed act as against chance effect.*

This process goes on for several days until, ultimately dissatisfied, Joan decides to abandon the painting—because, she says later, it is not specific enough; it lacks intensity and accuracy: she has failed. And so she drinks and smokes, in place of working. And then she drinks and smokes some more.

Sandler can't keep up with her; he is trying to write, to take notes, to stay sober—he has a job to do, a deadline to meet. He continues the interview while she is not painting. He asks her about color.

She shrugs and says, "I guess I would wish it not to be what Hofmann calls 'monotonous, that is, tonal and boring.'"

Then he asks about light.

"I hate it when it looks muddy (earthbound). Motion is important. But a movement should also sit still." Above all, she says, she must like her paintings. "I am not a member of the make-it-ugly school."

Gradually she gets back to work, forcing herself to paint—because she feels she has to, because Sandler is there—for the article. *Or because I'm a masochist*, she laughs.

But paint what? She tells him she needs a subject she likes in order to feel good enough to be able to work. Overnight, a friend has jokingly suggested that she paint her poodle named George, swimming. And so she does: "I had to think of something happy and someone I loved, so I thought of George," she says later; "Barney gave me George as his replacement. When he insisted on divorcing me, as he had on marrying me, he went to Paris and bought George, and he said a Frenchman was coming."

The painting begins with variations of intensity and saturation of the color yellow—sunlight, perhaps. But during the second all-night session, the work changes. The yellows turn to whites and the feeling becomes cold and bleak. Joan mentions a hurricane that hit the Hamptons in fall of 1954, and says that this is the fourth painting she has done based on that experience.

Storms were always threatening, she says now, alluding to her childhood on Lake Michigan. *They're always just off the water.*

"The painting has to work," she says, "but it has to say something more than that the painting works."

Now, she faces Sandler, faces the painting. And there it is, in front of the two of them—for *Art*

News readers, for posterity, but most of all for herself—the finished, working painting: *George Went Swimming at Barnes Hole, but It Got too Cold.*

George Went Swimming At Barnes Hole, But It Got Too Cold, 1957
Oil on canvas, 85 $^1/_4$ x 78 $^1/_4$ in.
Albright-Knox Art Gallery, Buffalo, New York

*The consciousness of the personal and sponta-
neous...stimulated the artist to invent devices of
handling, processing, surfacing, which confer to
the utmost degree the aspect of the freely made.
Hence the importance of the mark, the stroke, the
brush, the drip, the quality of the substance of
the paint itself, and the surface of the canvas as
a texture and field of operation —all signs of the
artist's active presence... The impulse...becomes
tangible and definite on the surface of a canvas
through the painted mark. We see, as it were, the
track of emotion, its obstruction, persistence or
extinction.*

—Meyer Schapiro

The
Twenty-four-year
Live-In

She first meets him in Paris in '55, in a Saint Germain café, with friends. *He,* is Jean-Paul Riopelle, the French-Canadian painter—a big, impulsive man with an even bigger appetite. There he is and there they collide and run together for twenty-four years.

He's married, has children, but he's also a painter, has a wry, dry sense of humor, says things like, *I'm not so much an Impressionist as a Depressionist.* That gets her. And he respects her work, too.

Before long, whenever she's in town, it's Joan and Jean-Paul; Frank O'Hara even couples them later in a poem ("Adieu Norman, Bonjour to Joan and Jean-Paul").

And so Joan begins dividing her time between New York and Paris, between her flat on St. Mark's Place—where Frank sometimes stays when she's abroad (out of which comes his poem

"At Joan's")—and studios on rue Jacob, rue Daguerre, and rue Decrés. In Paris, she misses New York badly, and in New York she misses Jean-Paul even worse, until they move into a studio together on rue Frémicourt in the fifteenth arrondissement. Though she will continue to visit and show in New York, from now on she will paint only in France.

LADY DAY
AND LADYBUG

A yellow leaflet with her face on it seen posted around the Village and in Chelsea—all over Manhattan, in fact. Frank is the first of their group to spot it and report back: Billie Holiday, in a midnight concert at the Loew's Sheridan, 7th Avenue and 12th Street: June 15, 1957. Everybody who's anybody knows that Lady Day hasn't played a club in Manhattan for about ten years, ever since she was denied a cabaret card after her drug bust and subsequent year in prison. But there's nothing saying she can't play a *theater* in Manhattan, and so she's booked at Loew's, the date co-sponsored by *The Village Voice* and Art d'Lugoff, owner of the Village Gate.

Frank tells everybody in his circle, but then comes the night of June 15th. Joe (LeSueur) says either that he can't or he won't stay up so late; and John (Ashbery) is in Paris... And so it goes. And in the end it's just Frank, Joan, and Mike Goldberg, along with their fellow abstract expressionist Norman Bluhm, and his girlfriend, actress Irma Hurley. They arrive at the theatre shortly before midnight, brimming with anticipation. Holding court as usual, Frank informs them that Edward Hopper painted the inside of the theatre back in 1937, says he's seen the painting. *Golden*, he adds, in his inimitable way, splaying his fingers and flashing his eyes, as if acting out the word.

But that was then. Now, twenty years later, the gold has tarnished and faded and the lighting is kept low to hide the shabbiness of the place. Twelve years from now the theatre will be shuttered for good; and in just over two years Lady Day will be dead and Frank will write one of his most famous lunch poems, "The Day Lady Died."

Joan is just back from Paris and carrying a flask of scotch, which she passes around.

Midnight comes and goes. Frank notices the tension between Joan and Mike but thinks little of it; there is Mike's instability, for starters, as well as the fact that Joan is already seeing Jean-Paul. He interrupts their quibbling to say that most of those in the audience seem like diehard fans, *So everybody probably knows that Lady is rarely on time.*

There are several opening acts—the Modern Jazz Quartet, Mingus and his Quintet, and others, to keep the crowd entertained and from becoming too restless.

But by 2:00 there's a stir in the crowd. The anticipation dissipates, is diluted: *Is she coming or not?* It's widely known among nighthawks that the city has a 3:00 A.M. entertainment curfew. Now word somehow spreads through the crowd that Lady had a gig in Philadelphia earlier that same evening and is on her way.

But people are getting antsy. Some leave. And in fact, Irma says she wants to go home and that she wants Norm to go with her. He runs a hand through his unruly, long black hair and rolls his eyes at the others, then lights another Gauloise.

Joan stares Irma down and says that she digs Lady, that she's always wanted to see her, that she's not budging an inch and that Bluhm shouldn't either. Frank and Mike concur.

And then, shortly before 3:00 A.M.—there she is, standing in a pin spotlight on the stage. She seems a little out of it at first, drunk or stoned, or both. But my god, is she beautiful. Handsome. Sleek. Tight, slinky dress. Hair pulled back in a ponytail. Dangling earrings. She is talking to the band, speech that is sometimes audible throughout the 2,500-seat theatre and sometimes not, depending upon her proximity to the microphone at any given moment. Her words are slurred, and Frank overhears someone behind him whispering that he'd heard Lady had a glass in hand when she got in the car in Philadelphia, and then insisted on stopping at a bar along the way.

Now she faces the audience, closes in on the microphone and finally begins to sing, and it's all over, man—all the doubt and discomfort, the sleepiness and the boredom, the tension or the lack thereof; it's all gone. And Joan and Mike and Frank and Bluhm—they're gone, too; even Irma is gone. Just GONE. Or rather they're HERE. Hard to say which. But what's for sure is that they're *with* Lady, who seems to be both absent and present at the same time. They're in her orbit. In her groove. She opens with *There Is No Greater Love*. And it is just so fucking sad, sad and eerie. But it is also—and there's no other word for it—beautiful.

Joan's feet are flat on her seat and her knees pulled up to her chest with her arms around them. It is as if she is perched, poised, both wrapped-up and rapt.

Lady fulfills her contract by singing for an hour, and then she performs two encores, closing as she always does in these last years and days, with *Strange Fruit*; by now it's 4:30.

As the five friends make their way out of the theatre, they decide to go out for an early breakfast. Frank, unable to resist repeating what he said after seeing Judy Garland at the Palace, says, *Well, I guess she's better than Picasso.*

That same year Joan paints "Ladybug," possibly her homage to Lady Day, with its rhythmic strokes of predominantly blues and greens and reds, its theatrical and—yes, let it be said—*intentional* drips, and its evocation of a line from Baudelaire: *A man who looks out of an open window never sees as much as a man who looks out of a closed one.*

Unpacking
Joan

She says, "I just think love has to do with painting—that's easy, no?"

And so—perhaps, thinking about her mother, and imagining the silence her mother lives with and how terrible it must be for her to no longer be able to *hear* poetry, that potentially glorious gumbo of words, Joan, in addition to taking up abstract painting as a way of escaping the constant competitiveness and criticism of her father, and because it is her *milieu*, the world in which she lives and who she is, also realizes it as a way to *give* to her mother, to herself—and also to the world, another kind of poetry, a visual poetry, as an expression of love, making the very act of painting all the more meaningful to her. Perhaps.

She says that her paintings are her feelings about something—Lake Michigan. Or water. Fields. Or her dogs. She says that they're more like a poem than anything.

And about Cézanne, one of her great loves, she says that his work "holds together: It is—there's nothing more to say. You can't read it. You can't wonder what it's about. It is."

And *Is*-ness is her business.

About her own work, she says, "I can't tell you what works. If I could say it in words, I'd write a book. It just works or it doesn't."

JOAN
AND JEAN-PAUL

Jean-Paul's outsized appetite includes a love for fast cars, fast boats, alcohol, and women. He speeds through the streets of Paris in his Bugatti or his Citröen, cruises the Mediterranean in the forty-five foot single-mast Bermuda cutter he owns a share in.

Or they'll sail with Pierre Matisse, the painter's son, and his wife Patricia. Joan doesn't like sailing, often stays below deck.

They drink a lot, fuck a lot, and fight a lot.

But they also paint a lot, always.

Beginning in the late 70s she has a poorly ventilated studio in Montparnasse that she keeps secret; she works on pastel drawings and sometimes sleeps there; a small bed occupies a loft space. It's hers and hers alone, away from home. And perhaps it's there that Beckett tells her, *Stick with Riopelle, he can fuck and I can't.*

She and Jean-Paul go on together.

MONARCHS

They are sailing to the island. It is a beautiful day, late September—sunny and cool, the wind is good. They will sail to the island, hike, eat lunch, and then return late afternoon and paint through the night. But one of them has forgotten the wine. And each blames the other.

Now he is angry. So is she. He seems to think it was her job to bring the wine, because she is the woman. This infuriates her. Of course he's mad at himself as well. As she is mad at herself. They yell at each other—back and forth they go. On and on. Then they fall silent: a boat is a small space to fight in.

The sail is uneventful, and quicker than usual: the wind at their back. Because he is the experienced sailor and the boat is his domain, he barks orders at her—obviously enjoying it. She does as he tells her but resents it like hell. Otherwise, they don't speak. Instead, the wind speaks for them—through the occasional violent slap of sails.

He drops anchor in the harbor, pulls the dory up beside them, and then, after some awkwardness about which of them will get in first (she can easily imagine him sailing away, leaving her there), they exchange hostile glances. In better times, and privately, he jokingly calls her *Rosa Malheur*, and she calls him, simply, *amour*. But not today. Today she hates him.

He hopes things will improve between them once they are on the island. And so he rows, furiously, to meet that future. On another day she would admire this fury. Before long, they are ashore. She gets out. He gets out. She walks off down the beach and lets him drag the dory in by himself. He ties it to a rock, and then they set off without a word.

The terrain of forest floor is soft to the foot, gives—it has been an unusually rainy September. She walks behind, following him, staring at his back, his broad shoulders, which she has looked up at countless times over the years. He doesn't bother to turn around to make sure she is keeping up. She feels only a blind hatred for him now, nothing more. Wild mushrooms, yellow and red, pepper the forest. She knows that those are the most poisonous kind and imagines reaching down, grabbing one with her fist, cramming it into her mouth and asphyxiating. But she doesn't. And wouldn't. Instead, they continue to walk, the ocean on their right, extending into the horizon, gently slapping rocks at the shoreline. The occasional monarch butterfly flits by.

They come to an opening that is high and flat and looks out over a wide span of sea. He gazes at her as if to ask if this is all right, if this pleases her majesty. He sits down without waiting for a response. She begins to sit, too, as she notices more and more butterflies. As she silently unpacks the bag with their bread, cheese, and fruit, lays it on the rock surface between them, suddenly, just to the right, she sees a whole school of monarchs: hundreds of them, lighting on a field of aster, their orange, black-veined wings shot through with sunlight—like stained-glass windows, vibrant against the lavender wildflowers. The edge of the forest, a green backdrop, is blanketed with goldenrod. The combination of colors entrances her. She leans forward, places both hands on the rock-floor to steady herself. She looks away, to clear her eyes and mind. She feels as though she could cry. It is a terrible beauty. She knows the arduous journey the butterflies have ahead of them, knows they are dying, that they live less than a year. She looks out at the ocean for refreshment: close-up, by the rocks, the water is a blue-green sea foam, aquamarine, white-capped, and then just beyond it begins to turn to a deeper, moodier blue. Indigo. She glances back to the feast of orange, black, lavender, mustard, shards of green, and she takes it all in, absorbs it. Deeper into the forest, the sunlight filtering through the trees is a lemony yellow. She lies down on the rock; wants to merge with it, to become one with the scene. She looks up at the sky, but it's all wrong—not the colors she'd hoped for: too weak and diluted. Now she looks at him—his back is to her, and he's wrong, too. And so she closes her eyes and begins the task of recreating the landscape, searing it into her mind.

I sometimes stopped to look at dried stains on the walls, loose ashes on the hearth, the transitory clouds and movements in a stream and if I closely gazed I would discover there contrivances galore.

—*How to Paint*, Leonardo da Vinci

JOAN
AND SAM

They often meet in a bar in Montparnasse called Rosebud.

Both loathe discussing their work. When they speak at all, it's economically, and after a few drinks, epigrammatically, and darker than night.

Barney once spent a day with them and said all they talked about was color. For hours. Mostly the color blue.

Sometimes Giacometti is there, too. As is Riopelle, jealous of their deep bond. Beckett has told Jean-Paul that he sees Joan as a younger version of another friend, because she expresses the same relentless quest for the void that he finds in that friend's paintings.

Some of his titles: *Not I*; *How It Is*; *The Unnameable*; *Nohow On*.

Some of hers: *Then, Last Time*; *Between*;
Another; *Before*.

It's 1970 and two-thirds of her life is over.

No Rain

Joan is in the studio painting on a midsummer night. The air outside is comfortable, easy. She is standing across the room from the huge canvas-in-progress, surveying what she has done and trying to determine what she will do next. She adjusts her glasses, lights up another cigarette, and fidgets with the thigh of her jeans. Beloved Marion, her German Shepherd named after Joan's mother, raises her head to watch her mistress as she moves from one side of the room to the other, approaches the canvas and then steps away from it, walking backward. Aware of the good dog's vigilance, Joan looks at her and asks, *What do you think, girl?* Marion cocks her head to the side, inquisitively, as if to say, *What?* Joan throws back her head and laughs.

In the background, on the stereo, Maria Callas as *Norma* is murdering her children. It is not because children are being murdered that Joan finds the music so compelling, but because of the passion, the depth of feeling in Callas's voice: that's what's fantastic; it's everything—she adores Callas. But Marion doesn't like opera, sometimes going so far as to cover her ears when it's playing. And because Joan thinks of Marion much as she did her mother, as a "tender companion," she considers changing the record to jazz for Marion's sake. Miles Davis maybe. She loves the colors he blows: "Blue in Green." Which takes her back to the painting.

Right now she's got a lot of lavender going—Canada. But she's also moving beyond Canada, away from Canada, as well as away from the Canadian (Riopelle), and onto something new—she's just not sure what yet. Black.... Green.... Blue....

She opens the studio door and feels glad it's not raining (as it has done so often of late), and the very same moment she has that thought, she realizes this is what she's feeling, and also what she's painting—*No Rain*.

La Vie en Rose

It was there from the start—always a lot of black, a big, near-solid boulder, obscurant. But she was looking through those damn tinted glasses, didn't see it, pushed it down. It wasn't just him, it was her too, their dynamic—but they respected each other as painters.

Over the years he told her this and that; he promised, and she forgot that she was viewing it all through a certain lens. Eventually and inevitably came the end, when he left her for the dog-sitter, and the black that was always there encroached—and the deathly white came, too.

And though she can't know that he will be devastated by her death, ten years before his own, and paint *Homage á Rosa Luxemburg* in her memory, we know that she still loved him, in her way.

She goes on.

La Vie en Rose, 1979
Oil on canvas, quadriptych, 110 1/8 x 268 1/4 in.
Metropolitan Museum of Art

STILL PAINTING

A terrible beauty. Yeats' phrase, isn't it? *What rough beast* and all that....

But the blank canvas, that's what's before her now. How and where to start?

Make a mark, just to get rid of that damn blank whiteness confronting you. Make a mark and then hope *something* comes to you—a feeling; a memory; a scene—*something*. She won't paint, can't paint, if she doesn't feel anything.

Drinking helps. As does smoking—or it's something to do with her hands anyway.

Reading poetry or listening to music helps, too.

But that mark—black on the canvas: or is it black? Could one begin with, say, yellow? Yes, and she has. So make a mark with yellow then: let it be sunlight; faded air; sunflowers; the sky after a storm; a wheat field.

She thinks of Van Gogh, whose work she's loved since she was a child, back when it was okay to love Van Gogh. Van Gogh standing in that damn wheat field, crows buzzing overhead and something else buzzing in his one good ear (the damn ear). The intensity of that seeing, those brushstrokes, standing all day in the hot sun - it's enough to drive anybody crazy.

But she doesn't work outside, doesn't stand in the middle of wheat fields, crows buzzing overhead, doesn't stand anywhere outside to paint for that matter, because she doesn't need to—or rather (not to put down Van Gogh or anybody else who paints *plein air*), it's just not the way she works. Her method is about distilling experience, about memory and feelings and not so much about the thing itself, rendered directly; it's about indirectness, about *after the fact*. It's very subjective. And retrospective.

She knows it probably sounds like bullshit but also knows it's not: she would prefer not to have to talk about it. She's been painting for forty-plus years and knows what she's doing. This is important because she believes that this knowing and experience has to come first, the trained hand

and eye, the knowledge of line and space, of color, the feel of paint, its thickness or thinness, the various brushes—when to lift the hand, to pause; which movement of the wrist to use here, there; when to flick or drip; when to brush, to saturate: how to translate feelings to the canvas. Look at Picasso's early work. Or even Pollock's. It takes years to get to the work they did later, and that she's been doing for a while now.

She's thinking too much. She can't, or she doesn't want to think when she paints. She just wants to feel it, whatever *it* is—the remembered experience, the *feeling*, and of course the paint itself, the brushes and the movement (her body). Good or bad, it doesn't matter; it's about feeling *something*. Not feeling anything is the worst. She can't paint then.

Being Alive

"When I was sick in the hospital they moved me to a room with a window and suddenly through the window I saw two fir trees in a park, and the gray sky, and the beautiful gray rain, and I was so happy. It had something to do with being alive. I could see the pine trees, and I felt I could paint. If I could see them, I felt I would paint a painting. Last year, I could not paint. For a while I did not react to anything. All I saw was a white metallic color."

"Feeling, existing, living, I think it's all the same, except for quality. Existing is survival; it does not necessarily mean feeling. You can say good morning, good evening. Feeling is something more: it's feeling your existence. It's not just survival. Painting is a means of feeling 'living.'... Painting is the only art form except still photography which is without time.... It never ends, it is the only thing that is both continuous and still.

Then I can be very happy. It's a still place. It's like one word, one image."

Blood on
the
Canvas

Often, throughout her life as a painter, she works in badly ventilated spaces, using powdery substances, including cadmium red. This is true even in later years, at her studio in Montparnasse, for example, true even when she's already having the lung problems that will eventually kill her. Those closest to her think she is hastening her own end, but then this is a woman for whom painting is life itself.

Faded Air

It is one of her most beautiful paintings (beautiful and true)—thinly applied, hectic black and green squiggles against a background of yellow and fading pink link the two panels of the diptych. It is also, perhaps, something of a self-portrait—painted between hospital stays, when she was having more and more trouble getting around, painting airy and thin because she didn't have the physical stamina.

Self as sunflower.

One gasps for breath, and then at the beauty of the painting.

This is about the failure of language, the limitation of words (the subtext of this project), which she knew so well: "I can't tell you what works. If I could say it in words..."

Faded Air, 1985
Oil on canvas, diptych, 102 x 102 in.
Collection of Thomas and Darlene Furst

The Color White

"It's death. It's hospitals. It's my terrible nurses. You can add in Melville, Moby Dick, a chapter on white. White is absolute horror, just horror. It is the worst."

... there yet lurks an elusive something in the innermost idea of this hue (white), *which strikes more of panic to the soul than that redness which affrights in blood.* - Moby Dick, Chapter 42: "The Whiteness of the Whale," Herman Melville.

"Painting without white would be like planting a garden without plants."

"In the early 1980s she said to an art historian that she felt closer to Agnes Martin's precise, sensitive, sensual abstraction than to the American expressionists. "

ENDGAME

Some younger artist friends drop by, hang out, talk shop—Joan now with pen always in hand, and sometimes in her mouth, replacing the endless cigarettes. In some ways life is easier, if not exactly easy—she is letting go of so much. It is a pleasure to give in, to give way, to give over, to be able to enjoy, to relax. It is not as easy for her to work as it used to be, though she does still work—and that's a good day.

She needs assistance now. Has to work fast, there isn't much time. Can't walk without a cane; her eyesight's failing; her hands painfully arthritic—can't unscrew the tops off paint tubes. And now when up on the ladder, something she's always done with the larger work, she's got to be hopeful: "I just get up on that fucking ladder and tell myself, This stroke has to work." And more often than not it does.

She's pleased with the little pastel from the other day. *No Birds*, an allusion to van Gogh's last painting, the one he was working on when he died—*Crows in a Wheat Field*.

She is near death, and she knows it—it has come on fast. October, and at home in Vétheuil, in the surrounding fields, the sunflowers are also dying. She pictures them—turning their heads away from the sun, fading, drooping, their petals folding in on themselves, drying up.... It is, as her old friend Sam would say, the endgame.

Briefly, she returns to America, flies to Manhattan one last time—to see friends, to work on some final prints in Westchester, to draw up her will, and to see the Matisse retrospective at the Museum of Modern Art.

Now back across the ocean, in Paris, in the hospital—her lungs are giving out. Everything possible is being done to make her comfortable.

There is far too much white in the room, and out her window—gray. But she will simply remember color and fill it in as she needs to, as she has done her entire life. Matisse's work—she's recently seen so much of it—works nicely from her bed; she imagines some of his cutouts, with the available light filtering through. And there are also the blues of Lake Michigan, the greens and yellows of Saugatuck, too: always have been.

A Few Days are all we have—her friend Jimmy Schuyler's poem. *So count them as they pass. They pass/too quickly....*

NOTES

Epigraphs

3 "Nearly 20 years": Jed Perl, in his review of *Joan Mitchell: Lady Painter, A Life*, by Patricia Albers. *The New York Times Book Review*, July 10, 2011.

9 "In a society that didn't allow abstract painting": Barney Rosset, in interview, in *Joan Mitchell*, Judith E. Bernstock (New York: Hudson Hills Press, in association with the Herbert F. Johnson Museum of Art, Cornell University, 1988).

9 "If Mitchell had had to choose": Klaus Kertess, in *Joan Mitchell* (Harry N. Abrams, New York, 1997), p. 29.

Big Joan/Little Joan

19 "They call me *sauvage*": Joan Mitchell, interviewed in Marion Cajori, director, *Joan Mitchell: Portrait of an Abstract Painter* (New York: Art

Kaleidoscope Foundation and Christian Black-wood Productions, 1992). Film.

20 "Big Joan/Little Joan": Ibid.

20 "Abandonment is also death": Joan Mitch-ell, in "Conversations with Joan Mitchell," Yves Michaud, *Joan Mitchell: New Paintings*, ed. Xavier Fourcade, (New York 1986), unpaginated.

20 "my twenty-four year live in": Joan Mitchell, interviewed in Marion Cajori, director, *Joan Mitchell: Portrait of an Abstract Painter* (New York: Art Kaleidoscope Foundation and Chris-tian Blackwood Productions, 1992). Film.

Skating

25 "A girl, her foot shod": Mary Gordon, in *Joan of Arc*, (New York: Viking, 2000), p. xx.

The Alphabet is Color

29 "a very self-made man": Joan Mitchell, inter-viewed in Marion Cajori, director, *Joan Mitchell: Portrait of an Abstract Painter* (New York: Art Kaleidoscope Foundation and Christian Black-wood Productions, 1992). Film.

30 "bluer than bleu": ": Ibid.

30 "If I could say it in words": Ibid.

31 "And bleakness comes through the trees": Ibid.

Rebel with a Cause

36 "Full of Jews": Joan Mitchell, interviewed by Linda Nochlin, "Tape-Recorded Interview with Joan Mitchell, April 16, 1986," transcript, Archives of American Art, Smithsonian Institution, Washington, D.C. pp. 15-16.

38 "a tender and sensitive companion": Joan Mitchell, in Catherine Flohic, in Flohic et al., *Ninety : Art des Anneés 90/Art in the 90s. Joan Mitchell,* no. 10 (Paris: Eighty Magazine, 1993), p. 3.

Painting

43 "You carried death around with you": Joan Mitchell, in interview, in *Joan Mitchell,* Judith E. Bernstock (New York: Hudson Hills Press, in association with the Herbert F. Johnson Museum of Art, Cornell University, 1988).

43 "Really Frenchy": Joan Mitchell, interviewed by Linda Nochlin, "Tape-Recorded Interview with Joan Mitchell, April 16, 1986," transcript, Ar-

chives of American Art, Smithsonian Institution, Washington, D.C., p. 7.

44 "I carry the landscape around with me": Joan Mitchell, interviewed in Marion Cajori, director, *Joan Mitchell: Portrait of an Abstract Painter* (New York: Art Kaleidoscope Foundation and Christian Blackwood Productions, 1992). Film.

Leaving Chicago

46 "I left Chicago in the middle": Joan Mitchell, interviewed in Lyn Blumental/Kate Horsfield directors, *Joan Mitchell: An Interview* (Chicago), Video Data Bank, 1974). Film.

48 "He was talking about the push": Joan Mitchell, in *Joan Mitchell*, Judith E. Bernstock (New York: Hudson Hills Press, in association with the Herbert F. Johnson Museum of Art, Cornell University, 1988), p. 17.

49 "Mitchell, you should be painting'": Joan Mitchell, interviewed by Linda Nochlin, "Tape-Recorded Interview with Joan Mitchell, April 16, 1986," transcript, Archives of American Art, Smithsonian Institution, Washington, D.C. p. 21.

Mexico

51 "Nobody talks about Mexico": Barney Rosset, interview with Siri Huvestedt, "Joan Mitchell: Remembering in Color," in *Mysteries of the Rectangle: Essays on Painting* (New York: Princeton Architectural Press, 2005), 140.

51 "I had been in love with Mexico": Joan Mitchell, interviewed by Linda Nochlin, "Tape-Recorded Interview with Joan Mitchell, April 16, 1986," transcript, Archives of American Art, Smithsonian Institution, Washington, D.C., p. 12.

Paris

54 "They don't seem to laugh": Joan Mitchell, letter to Barney Rosset, in "Remembering Joan," *Evergreen Review* #104, Spring/Summer 2001.

54 "Cubing it up": Joan Mitchell, in *Originals: American Women Artists*, Eleanor Munro (New York: Simon & Schuster), p. 244.

Manhattan

60 "I'd listen and we'd drink": Joan Mitchell, interviewed in Lyn Blumental/Kate Horsfield directors, *Joan Mitchell: An Interview* (Chicago), Video Data Bank, 1974). Film.

61 "Everything Joan did": Mary Gordon, in *Joan of Arc*, (New York: Viking, 2000), pp. 142-143.

The Obstacle Race

64 "Joan, if only you were French, and male, and dead": Joan Mitchell, interviewed in Marion Cajori, director, *Joan Mitchell: Portrait of an Abstract Painter* (New York: Art Kaleidoscope Foundation and Christian Blackwood Productions, 1992). Film.

Still a Small World for Women

67 "What was it like to be a woman": Joan Mitchell, interviewed by Linda Nochlin, "Tape-Recorded Interview with Joan Mitchell, April 16, 1986," transcript, Archives of American Art, Smithsonian Institution, Washington, D.C., p. 21.

67 "Well, you got shows in those days": Joan Mitchell, in *Originals: American Women Artists*, Eleanor Munro (New York: Simon & Schuster), p. 246.

67 "The men helped me more than the women": Ibid.

67 "When I was discouraged": Joan Mitchell, interviewed by Linda Nochlin, "Tape-Recorded

Interview with Joan Mitchell, April 16, 1986," transcript, Archives of American Art, Smithsonian Institution, Washington, D.C., p. 21.

67 "The galleries had quota systems": Ibid.

67 "I would have had a lot easier time": Ibid, p. 22.

68 "Frankenthaler? You mean that tampon painter?": Joan Mitchell, interviewed by Mark Stevens and Annalyn Swan, in *De Kooning: An American Master* (Knopf, New York, 2005) p. 345.

George Went Swimming at Barnes Hole, but It Got too Cold

All quotes attributed to Joan Mitchell in this chapter (pages 78 - 84) are from Irving Sandler's invaluable "Mitchell Paints a Picture," *ArtNews* 56:6 (October 1957): 44-47, 69-70.

"New York School"

"Hardening of the categories causes art disease"

"No, I spend too much time looking, which stops action"

"Not much. I am too traditional"

"An avant-garde is by definition dated"

"Crudeness and accuracy"

"He wore spats, a morning coat and carried a cane"

"A bridge to me is beautiful"

"I paint from a distance"

"I guess I would wish it not to be what Hofmann"

"I hate it when it looks muddy (earthbound"

"I had to think of something happy and someone I loved"

"The painting has to work"

85 The consciousness of the personal and spontaneous": Meyer Schapiro, in "Recent Abstract Paintings, 1957, in *Modern Art: 19th and 20th Centuries* (London: Chatto & Windus, 1978) p. 222.

The Twenty-four-year Live-In

88 "I'm not so much an Impressionist as a Depressionist": Jean-Paul Riopelle, quoted in *The Toronto Globe and Mail*. With reports from Canadian Press and Reuters, March 14, 2002 – Page R1

Lady Day and Ladybug

95 "Well, I guess she's better than Picasso": Frank O'Hara, in *City Poet: The Life and Times of Frank O'Hara*, Brad Gooch (Knopf, New York, 1994), p. 327.

Unpacking Joan

97 "I just think love has to do with painting": Joan Mitchell, interviewed in Marion Cajori, director, *Joan Mitchell: Portrait of an Abstract Painter* (New York: Art Kaleidoscope Foundation and Christian Blackwood Productions, 1992). Film

97 "My paintings are my feelings": Ibid.

98 "Cézanne's work holds together": Ibid.

98 "I can't tell you what works": Ibid.

Joan and Jean-Paul

100 "Stick with Riopelle": Samuel Beckett, quoted in *Samuel Beckett: The Last Modernist*, by Anthony Cronin (Harper, New York, 1994) p. 433.

Being Alive

122 "When I was sick in the hospital": Joan

Mitchell, in "Conversations with Joan Mitchell," Yves Michaud, *Joan Mitchell: New Paintings*, ed. Xavier Fourcade, (New York 1986), unpaginated.

122 "Feeling, existing, living": Ibid.

Faded Air

127 "I can't tell you what works": Joan Mitchell, interviewed in Marion Cajori, director, *Joan Mitchell: Portrait of an Abstract Painter* (New York: Art Kaleidoscope Foundation and Christian Blackwood Productions, 1992). Film

The Color White

130 "It's death. It's hospitals": Joan Mitchell, in *Abstract Expressionism*, Barbara Hess, (Taschen, Köln, 2006), p. 78.

130 "Painting without white": Joan Mitchell, in *Joan Mitchell*, Judith E. Bernstock (New York: Hudson Hills Press, in association with the Herbert F. Johnson Museum of Art, Cornell University, 1988), n.p.

130 "felt closer to Agnes Martin's": Joan Mitchell, in Catherine Flohic, in Flohic et al., *Ninety : Art des Anneés 90/Art in the 90s. Joan Mitchell*, no. 10 (Paris: Eighty Magazine, 1993), p. 3.

Endgame

132 "I just get up on that fucking ladder": Joan Mitchell. In conversation with Klaus Kertess, spring 1992. *Joan Mitchell*, Klaus Kertess, Harry N. Abrams, 1997, (p. 40).

134 "A few days are all we have": James Schuyler, *A Few Days* (Random House, New York, 1985).

Photo

135 Photograph of Joan Mitchell © 2015 Estate of Rudy Burckhardt / Artists Rights Society (ARS), New York

ACKNOWLEDGEMENTS

The long journey that ended with this book began when I first saw Marion Cajori's film *Joan Mitchell: Portrait of an Abstract Painter* at the Museum of Fine Arts in Boston in 1993: I fell in love with the brilliant, fascinating, complex Mitchell; I had long admired her work. I spoke with Marion Cajori a year before her death in August 2006 and she could not have been more gracious: she did the world a great favor by making the film. The Whitney Museum's glorious 2002 retrospective pushed me over the edge, and work on this project began a few years later.

Many people were helpful to me in numerous ways during (and after) the writing, some providing important research material, others sharing my passion for Mitchell's work, and still others offering technical expertise and/or emotional support: I couldn't have written this book without them. Thanks first and foremost to my partner, Lee Salkovitz, who accompanied me all over the map to take in Mitchell's work and who shares my love for it; thanks also to my ever-supportive sisters, Marcia Kay Lippincott and Cindy Lippincott Brown.

Thanks to Bruce Aufhammer, Verna Austen, Joseph Caldwell, Ted Chiles & Chella Courington, Mary Clyde, Kristin Matly Dennis, Troy Ehlers, Eileen Fitzpatrick, Foust, Kirby Gann & Stephanie Tittle, Margery Gans, Gayle & George Hanratty, Martha Harrison, Michael Higgins, Hyewon Hyun, Sharona Jacobs, Anthony James, Bradford Johnson, Liza Mattison, Cate McGowan, Terry McKinney, Eleanor Morse, Sena Naslund, John Neely, Lesléa Newman, Loreen Niewenhuis, Bob Olive, Erin Reid, Jamie Sieger and Jim Isaacs, Rosanna Staffa, AshleyRose Sullivan, Laura van den Berg, Neela Vaswani, Karen Watson, Julia Watts, Jan Mattingly-Weintraub, and Crystal Wilkinson. Thanks also to the late Carl Plansky, to the late Bob O'Handley, to Carol O'Handley, and to my late editor at Viking, Ray Roberts.

And thanks, of course, to my collaborator Laura S. Jones/Tidal Press, for loving and publishing this book.

Numerous books and articles were invaluable to me in one way or another during my work on this project. They are listed here in no particular order. *The Paintings of Joan Mitchell*, Jane Livingston; *Joan Mitchell*, Klaus Kertess; *Originals: American Women Artists*, Eleanor Munro; *Joan Mitchell*, Judith Bernstock; "Mitchell Paints a Picture," Irving Sandler, *Art News*, October 1957; *The Sweeper-Up After Artists*, Irving Sandler; *City Poet: The Life and Times of Frank O'Hara*, Brad Gooch; *Joan of Arc*, Mary Gordon; *De Kooning: An American Master*, Mark Stevens and Annalyn Swan; "Remembering in Color," from *Mysteries of the Rectangle*, Siri Huvstedt; "My Black Paintings," from *Serious Pink*, Shannon Dolin; *Unnatural Wonders: Essays from the Gap Between Art and Life*, Arthur Danto; *Digressions on Some Poems by Frank O'Hara*, Joe LeSueur; Video Data Bank, *Joan Mitchell: An Interview,* by Lyn Blumenthal and Kate Horsfield, 1974; Smithsonian Archives of American Art: Interview with Joan Mitchell, by Linda Nochlin; *Memories Arrested in Space*, Martin Gray; "Van Gogh: The Man Suicided by Society," Antonin Artaud; *Reported Sightings*, John Ashbery; *Art In Its Own Terms: Selected Criticism, 1935-1975*, Fairfield Porter;

The Party's Over: Reminiscences of the 50s, John Gruen; *New York in the Fifties*, Dan Wakefield; "Barney and Joan," Richard Milazzo, *Evergreen Review* ("Remembering Joan") #104; *Letters on Cezanne*, Rainer Maria Rilke; *In Memory of My Feelings: Frank O'Hara and American Art*, Russell Ferguson; as well as much of John Berger's work (especially *And Our Hearts, Our Faces, Brief as Photos*), Geoff Dyer's *But Beautiful: A Book About Jazz*, Michael Ondaatje's *Coming Through Slaughter* (as well as his example), and the work of Anne Carson. Though my book was finished before Patricia Albers' fine biography of Mitchell, *Lady Painter*, was released, I salute it, and her.

About the Author

Robin Lippincott has published three novels—*In the Meantime, Our Arcadia,* and *Mr. Dalloway,* as well as a collection of short stories, *The 'I' Rejected.* His fiction and nonfiction have appeared in *The Paris Review, Fence, Bloom, American Short Fiction, Memorious,* and many other journals; for ten years he wrote reviews of mostly art and photography books for *The New York Times Book Review.* He has held fellowships at Yaddo and the MacDowell Colony. Robin lives in the Boston area, and teaches in Spalding University's low residency MFA in Writing Program. His new book, *Rufus + Syd,* a young adult novel co-written with Julia Watts, will be published in spring 2016.